CAROL ARMSTRONG

Cats in Quilts

14 Purrfect Projects

C&T PUBLISHING

© 2002 by Carol Armstrong

Editors: Cyndy Lyle Rymer, Stacy Chamness
Technical Editor: Karyn Hoyt-Culp
Copy Editors/Proofreaders: Lucy Grijalva,
    Stacy Chamness, Carol Barrett
Cover Designer: Kristen Yenche
Book Designer: Rose Sheifer
Design Director: Diane Pedersen
Illustrator: Kirstie L. McCormick
Production Assistant: Kristy A. Konitzer
Photography: Sharon Risedorph unless
    otherwise noted
Published by C&T Publishing, Inc., P.O. Box
1456, Lafayette, California 94549

Front cover: Ollie Playing in the Pansies
Back cover: Jake Prowling in the Salvia; Molly,
Sassy, and the Tulips

Library of Congress Cataloging-in-Publication Data
Armstrong, Carol,
    Cats in quilts : 14 purrfect projects / Carol Armstrong.
        p. cm.
    ISBN 1-57120-175-0 (paper trade)
    1. Appliqué--Patterns. 2. Quilting--Patterns. 3. Cats
in art. I. Title.
TT779 .A758 2002   746.46'041—dc21
    2002000980

Printed in China
10 9 8 7 6 5 4

CONTENTS

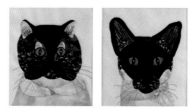

Dedicated to Gardeners and Cat Lovers Everywhere

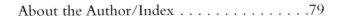

Introduction

Meow! These furry friends, full of personality, have come to visit the garden. What great fun these cats are to appliqué along with the colorful blooms. Piece by piece, they come alive with character as you sew.

Using my no-fuss, no-template, lightbox-appliqué method, you will enjoy the process of creating cats and flowers in hand appliqué. Celebrate the little individual changes that always occur and let them become part of the finished design. Nature—and handwork—are ever changing. Leaves bend, petals fall, and kittens don't stay still at all.

Learn to be free with random, expressive quilting designs. Let those lines of quilting convey a mood, echo the appliqué, or add elements of sun, breezes, or floating clouds. Experiment, express yourself, and delight in the possibilities.

My relaxed techniques are a great place to begin your venture into hand appliqué and quilting. For those of you already bitten by the sewing bug, let this book broaden your horizons. Hand stitching all types of cats, along with a variety of garden flowers, will soothe the soul and make you smile inside and out.

Supplies

The following is a list of the basic tools and materials you will need to create cats and wildflowers in hand appliqué and quilting. Your investment of time deserves good quality materials for the best results. Taking a trip to your local quilt shop or turning the pages of a quilt supply catalog are good ways to get started.

TOOLS

Lightbox: The lightbox is integral for template-free appliqué. Quick and easy tracing of appliqué pieces, patterns, and designs is possible with this handy item. Lightboxes are available in many sizes at craft and art stores. In a pinch, use a window on a bright day or a small lamp under a glass table.

Cutting Tools: Sharp scissors are important; a large pair for cutting out fabric, and a small pair that cuts down to the points for snipping threads. A cutting mat, rotary or acrylic ruler, and rotary cutter are excellent for rapidly cutting border and binding strips, as well as squaring backgrounds.

Needles and Pins: For appliqué, I use a #10 milliner's needle. The extra length helps with needle-turning the seam allowances.

For basting, a long, regular sewing needle will serve you well.

For quilting, my choice is a #10 sharps. Many quilters like the shorter betweens needle.

Large-eyed embroidery needles are best for stitching details with floss.

As with many things, the needle that works best for you is the right one.

Pins give you an extra hand. For appliqué, short, ¾" glass-headed pins will hold but not be in the way. Longer silk pins or fine, long appliqué pins work well for pinning seams for borders or adding bindings.

Thimble: The styles available are endless. I use a small leather thimble on the pushing finger when quilting. Try many until you find which type, which finger, and at what times a thimble works best for you. Remember, all thimbles feel awkward at first.

Iron: A little steam and a little heat work wonders, so a good steam iron is an essential tool. A padded surface such as a folded towel works well for appliqué.

Markers: Removable fabric markers are part of the process. Water-removable blue markers are good, as are white, silver, or yellow pencils. Air-erasable purple markers work if you are going to sew at that moment, but note that they sometimes disappear quickly. The basic rules to follow when using any marker are: Mark lightly, do not iron over any marks, and test for removability. Marks should come out with just a little water. Check at your local guild or craft shop for the many options.

MATERIALS

Threads: For appliqué, use a good cotton or cotton-wrapped polyester thread. Select a color that closely matches the fabric to be appliquéd.

HINT   Natural light is best for matching colors.

For quilting, I use a natural-color quilting thread for unbleached muslin backgrounds as well as for large appliqué areas. You may also like to try different colors for cat body quilt lines or even for background quilting. I have used many brands with equal success.

For basting, a pure white multipurpose thread is best.

For embroidery, use good-quality embroidery floss. You will use many colors for the details on the flowers and cats. This little bit of extra detail really adds a lot to the finished appliqué designs.

Batting: I have found that a needle-punched polyester batting works best for showing off my quilting stitch. Specifically, I use Polyfil Traditional™ needle-punched batting.

Fabric: A quilter never has enough! For backgrounds and backing, I use 100% cotton, premium-quality unbleached muslin, pre-shrunk and with a crease-resistant finish. It's a good foundation for appliqué and a great fabric to show off quilted designs.

For hand appliqué, 100% cotton fabrics are the most cooperative. They needle-turn easily and respond well to finger-pressing, but, best of all, they come in so very, very many colors and prints. For those of us with an appetite for yummy fabrics, quilt shops and catalogs are serving up a feast!

I do not prewash my fabrics for wallhangings, but I do test for colorfastness by rinsing a scrap in lukewarm water to see if the color runs. If it does run, I rinse the entire piece of fabric until the water is clear. If you plan to wash the finished quilt project, you may wish to prewash the fabrics.

When choosing fabrics, note the weight and thickness of the cloth. There are some quilting cottons that, while excellent for borders, binding, or piecing, are not very friendly to appliqué due to their weight. However, sometimes I will work with a not-so-friendly fabric because it is the perfect color. Be flexible.

Color: For appliquéing flowers and cats, I use a mix of solid colors, subtle tone-on-tone prints, and other quiet prints. Note that the line formed by two appliqué pieces is a part of the drawing. If you were to use very busy or loud prints together, this line would be lost, as would part of your picture. Choosing fabrics takes a bit of practice and a lot of individual taste. I usually cut out all my appliqué pieces first to see how my chosen fabrics work. Often I will make some changes. The rejected pieces often work for smaller cuts in another project.

For cats, look for fabric designs that resemble cat fur, shadowed tone-on-tones, and some solid colors in the same family. For flowers and leaves, mottled colors or prints with leaves work well. Use your own preferences to create your personal fabric stash.

HINT Sometimes a large print works when cutting out small pieces, as the overall design is disguised. Do not discount the back of some fabrics for that perfect color.

Specialty Fabrics: Although I have appliquéd some eyes with cotton fabrics, the small pieces can prove difficult for beginning fingers. One solution is to use a faux suede fabric which comes in different weights and colors. This material does not fray, so eyes can be cut out to size and set in place with fabric glue. The "suede" also accepts markers and paints. See page 18 for more about eyes.

Extras: I use fabric glue for some eye construction. There are many brands of glue available. For coloring eyes, I use permanent markers, as well as fabric paints. There is lots of room for creativity here so feel free to experiment and play with various materials.

Lightbox Appliqué: The Method

Simple is easy; easy is fun, and fun is what you have when you appliqué the lightbox way. Why? Because with a lightbox there is no need for templates or freezer-paper cut-outs. The relaxed technique is "purrfect" for these adorable cats and bright garden flowers.

GENERAL INSTRUCTIONS

Draw your appliqué design on lightweight white paper with a black marker. Secure the drawing on the lightbox with a few pieces of masking tape. If your drawing is larger than your lightbox, tape the pattern to the reverse side of the background fabric instead. Then move the pattern and background as one on the lightbox. Remove the pattern from the fabric after the entire pattern is marked.

Your background fabric should be cut at least 1" larger all around than the final size needed. This allows any drawing up in the fabric to be corrected after the appliqué and embroidery has been completed and the piece pressed. Lay the background fabric, right side up, over the drawing on the lightbox. Secure with a few pins if you like. Using a water-removable marker, trace the entire design onto the background. (If you are experienced and sure of your appliqué ability, you can mark the design with a fine-line permanent marker such as a Pigma pen, but these lines must be covered entirely!) Remove the background from the lightbox but not the pattern. If the pattern is larger than the lightbox, remove the pattern from the back of the background fabric and place the pattern on the lightbox.

Using the pattern on the lightbox, trace each individual appliqué the exact finished size on the right side of your chosen appliqué fabric. Use a removable marker in a color that is clearly visible on the fabric. This line will be your guide for turning under the seam allowance. If another piece will overlap this piece, such as a leaf or a stem across a cat leg, mark these areas with a dotted line to aid in the placement of the overlapping pieces.

Cut out the marked pieces ³⁄₁₆" to ¼" outside the marked line. (Do not cut out the fabric areas that will be overlapped.) The allowance can be cut even larger and trimmed as you appliqué if it is in the way. This excess is helpful when there are many overlapping pieces, as with a cat. If a piece shifts a little, the extra fabric is there if needed or may be trimmed if not.

HINT   If you cannot see the pattern line through the fabric, try a red marker over the black line, a bit wider than the original line.

HINT   If you are appliquéing a light-color piece, you can add a lining to keep the turn-under allowance from showing through. Cut a lining patch the exact finished size of the appliqué (without the turn-under allowance) from a solid color that matches the appliqué fabric. Place the patch behind the appliqué piece and stitch as usual.

Begin stitching, using the numbers on the pattern for the order to appliqué. Those pieces that are covered by another piece are sewn down first. The lines you marked on the background fabric will be your guides. As you stitch, turn under the allowance with the needle, matching the line on the appliqué piece with the line on the background. Check often to

see that the piece is lined up correctly. On a large appliqué piece, pin the entire piece in place, turning under the allowance here and there to help line it up and to prevent stretching the piece as you sew. Turn under and sew only those edges that are exposed, not those that will be covered by another piece. Exception: If you are appliquéing a piece that will be over-lapped by a leaf or flower (such as another leaf, blade of grass, stem, tail, etc.) and the distance is short, turn under the allowance and keep stitching the entire piece to keep the lines smooth. For example, for the most part, the cats are appliquéd completely behind the leaves and flowers.

The markings you have made are removable, so don't worry about the little variations that occur. Being off a bit on overlapping pieces is fine, as long as all the raw edges are turned or covered by another piece. A short leaf, a bent stem, or a ruffle in cat fur is not a problem. Look at your appliqué picture as a whole, not at each individual piece. The marks disappear with a bit of water. Close is good. Enjoy the process.

When the appliqué is finished, embroider the details—such as stamens, whiskers, eyes, or eyebrows—on the flowers and cat. Remove any visible marks and allow the piece to dry completely. Press the appliqué from the back on a padded surface, using an iron with a bit of steam, set on a cotton setting. Trim the background to the required size.

HINT   On the larger cat body areas, you may trim the background away on the back if you like. I do not. I quilt through the extra layer with no problems, just fewer stitches at a time. This is your choice.

APPLIQUÉ ORDER

The appliqué pieces that are in the background of a design are sewn first. Each shape in the patterns is numbered by order of appliqué. With some experience, you will easily note the order yourself. Unnumbered pieces or those without overlaps can be sewn at any time.

PRE-APPLIQUÉ

This method of appliqué should be added to everyone's repertoire of appliqué techniques. This method improves the appearance of many designs and makes positioning motifs easier. With basic appliqué, pieces are stitched one at a time to the background. The pre-appliqué technique involves stitching a partial or entire motif *before* it is appliquéd to the background. A two-tone blade of grass or part of a cat ear might be stitched this way, or an entire face or flower. As you become more experienced with appliqué, you will naturally notice when this method is more effective.

The basic guidelines of appliqué still apply: same stitch, same marking, and generally the same order of appliqué. Appliqué each piece to the next, referring to the pattern.

Note: Do *not* stitch into the turn-under allowance. If left free, the seam allowance will turn under more easily when you appliqué the motif to the background.

Clip curves and trim excess fabric as needed. Remember to match the thread color to the appliqué fabric as you sew. Keep needles pre-threaded for convenience.

When your motif is complete, or a portion of a motif is ready, stitch it to the background as usual. The effectiveness of this method becomes more apparent as you gain experience with appliqué.

Pre-Appliqué

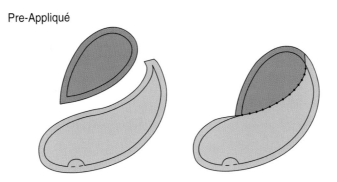

THE APPLIQUÉ STITCH

Thread a needle with a 12" to 18"-long single strand of thread in a color to match the appliqué (not the background fabric). A longer thread will wear and fray before you have used it all. Knot the end of the thread.

Whenever possible, begin your appliqué at one end of the shape to create a continuous line of stitching.

Keep the background fabric somewhat taut as you appliqué to avoid pushing the background fabric along with the appliqué piece. I appliqué on my lap, and for most projects the friction of the fabric on my jeans is enough to provide a smooth working background. If the background is small, however, or I am working at the edge of a piece, I may pin the background to my jeans or to a small lap pillow. Re-pin the background as you sew and need to turn the piece. Whenever you need an extra hand, try using more pins.

Using the shaft of the needle, turn under the edge of the piece at the marked line. Slip the knot into the fold of the turn-under by running the needle through the fold from the back of the appliqué piece and out onto the edge to be stitched down. The knot will be hidden in the fold.

Hold the appliqué in the marked place on the background. Insert the needle into the background, even with the thread's exit from the appliqué piece.

With the needle still under the background, move the needle tip forward. Come up through the background and through a few threads on the folded edge of the appliqué piece. Pull the thread snug without drawing up the fabric.

Again, insert the needle into the background even with the thread's last exit point from the turned edge. Travel a bit under the background, and come back up through the background, catching a few threads on the folded edge. Keep folding the turn-under allowance with the shaft of the needle as you go, trimming if necessary.

The appliqué stitch

To keep your stitching consistent and comfortable, turn your work as you sew. Do not work too far ahead of yourself. Now and then, check that the piece will line up with the lines marked on the background. Relax as you stitch. Let the little variations happen and create a wonderful appliqué design.

To end, secure the thread by taking three stitches in the same place in the background, behind the appliqué, or in an adjacent area of background that will be covered by another appliqué.

Practice will make you more comfortable with the needle, fabric, and technique. Soon your stitches will be small, even, and automatic.

INSIDE POINTS

Using your small embroidery scissors, clip to the inside point, just shy of the marked turn-under line. Avoid starting at the inside point. Start stitching the piece at a comfortable place that will give you a continuous line of stitching. Stitch almost to the inside point, but turn under all the way to the clip.

Using the needle, turn under part of the allowance on the opposite side, down to the clip. Hold in place.

Put the needle under the appliqué and pivot, rolling the allowance under and around the point. Hold in place, and stitch to the inside point. Take one or more tiny stitches at the inside point, then adjust the turn-under on the way out of the inside point, smoothing and stretching as necessary. Continue stitching around the piece.

Sewing an inside point

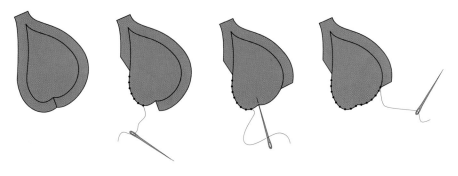

INSIDE CURVE

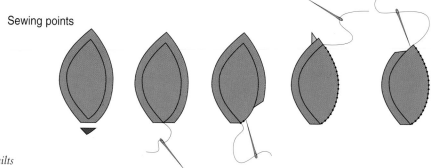

Clip the turn-under allowance as many times as needed for a smooth turn-under. Clip to within 1–2 threads before you reach the seam line. When the curves are tight, use the same pivoting needle technique you used for inside points.

I try to avoid creating tight curves or inside points whenever possible. A bit of practice on some scrap fabric is recommended.

Clipping inside curves

POINTS

Once you have sewn a few points, you will find that they are not so difficult. The sharper the point, the slower you should sew, carefully easing under the seam allowance. Try a few on practice fabric, and you'll soon be a pro.

Square off the end of the point, leaving a ³⁄₁₆" turn-under allowance. If there is too much fabric to turn under, simply trim it. Fold under the allowance straight across the point. Bring your thread up through the exact point, hiding the knot in the fold. Take one stitch into the background.

Hold down the end of the appliqué. Using the shaft of the needle, turn under a portion of the allowance beyond the point, and then stitch. Continue stitching to the next point. Make a stitch at the exact point on your appliqué shape. Take another tiny second stitch to secure the piece. Clip the excess fabric at the point. Push the seam allowance under using your needle, and stitch. Continue stitching to finish the piece.

There! You have now sewn a beginning point and a point within a line of stitching. Remember, not all points will be perfect, but nature allows for these imperfections.

Sewing points

BIAS STRIPS

Use fabric cut on the bias when stitching blades of grass or thin stems or branches. Bias is cut at a 45° angle to the straight grain. It does not fray easily, and is flexible enough to go around curves.

Bias strips

For stitching larger widths of bias, simply cut your bias strip the width of the finished appliqué plus the turn-under allowance on both sides. For example, cut a bias strip 1¼" wide for a ¾"-wide finished stem. Finger-press the allowance along one side, and stitch in place following the marked lines on the background. Use your needle to turn under the allowance along the other side as you stitch. I sew the inside edge of a curve first.

Tiny Bias Technique

For narrow bias strips, especially flower stems, I cut the strip about ½" wide so it will be easy to work with. As with wider strips, finger-press one side and stitch in place, using a ⅛" seam allowance, following your marked design. Flip the piece open to expose the turn-under allowance, and carefully trim the allowance close to the stitching, leaving enough fabric to secure the piece. Flip the piece back and trim to double the width needed for the stem. Needle-turn the allowance as you stitch down the other side. Some fabrics are more cooperative than others; if one fabric gives you trouble, try another piece. You will be surprised how narrow a line you can create with just a little practice.

Tiny bias

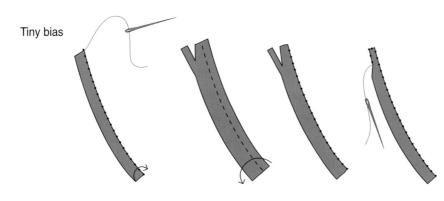

CAT EYES

The eyes add a lot of personality and attitude to these cats. Often the final results surprise and delight me as fabric, embroidery, or paint change a bit here and there in the construction. Cat eyes can be created in many ways. Following are several methods to use alone or in combination. Choose the style that best suits your level of experience or your aesthetic preference.

Appliquéd Eyes

This is the most challenging method because the pieces are so tiny, but there is fun in the challenge. Some eyes are completely appliquéd, while others are appliqué combined with embroidery or paint. Pre-appliqué (see page 12) is used for some eye parts. Go slowly with the small pieces, and if an eye is not to your liking, try again. (They use only a tiny bit of fabric.) Read through some of the projects to get an idea of where appliquéd eyes might work best; notice the eyes on page 34.

Embroidered Eyes

Eyes can be partially or entirely embroidered. Add an embroidered iris to a simple, appliquéd black eye shape, or outline a cut-out eye with a border or stem stitch to add depth and definition. A few stitches of white floss in the pupil of any eye adds sparkle.

You can completely finish the edges of an eye area and embroider the entire eye using a satin stitch. An eye may also be embroidered on a separate piece of fabric, cut out with a regular turn-under allowance, and appliquéd in place. There are many combinations, and the choice is yours.

Cut-Out Eyes

Cut-out eyes are by far the easiest eyes to create, and they look great! I prefer faux suede for these peepers. Use one or two layers of colored suede, or color your own using permanent markers or paint. Simply cut out the eye the exact size needed and add the iris and pupil dot, or cut an iris and pupil of suede and glue them onto the base of the eye.

Make sure the eye area of the appliqué is anchored securely. After the background has been pressed, attach the eyes with fabric glue, and allow the glue to dry completely before handling the piece. Because faux suede does not unravel, you can have a lot of fun cutting and creating eyes much as you would with paper. See what you can do with some "practice" eyes.

Again, I suggest you review some of the projects to see how I have constructed various eyes, and use the style you prefer on any cat. Alterations may be made to suit the technique you want to use. Do not hesitate to play. Fabric is willing to work with you.

EMBROIDERY

Embroidery is wonderful for those little details that are too small for appliqué, but which add so much to the finished picture. Use a hoop if you prefer. Unless otherwise noted, I use two strands of embroidery floss. The following basic stitches are used in the projects.

French Knot

A great highlight for flowers, the French knot may be clustered in the center of the flower, or used singly at the end of a stamen. You can increase the size of the knot by using more strands of floss.

Bring the needle up from the wrong side of the fabric. Wrap the floss around the needle twice, and insert the needle back into the fabric close to the thread's exit. Pull the needle through the fabric, holding the knot until all the floss is pulled through. Pull the knot, but not too tightly.

French knot

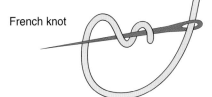

Stem Stitch

This simple stitch outlines eyes and makes delicate whiskers with only one strand of floss. Use it also for flower stamens and stems.

This stitch is worked left to right in slightly curved stitches. To make a line thicker, stitch two or more lines next to one another.

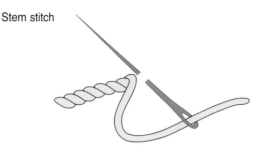

Stem stitch

Satin Stitch

Satin stitch

Use this stitch for coloring areas such as pupils or irises in the cat's eyes, to replace appliqué for the nostrils on those cute pink noses, or for filling in a mouth. Satin stitch can also create butterfly bodies or provide coverage for any area you need to fill with color.

Use straight stitches across the shape to be filled. Keep the stitches close together and as short as possible.

Borders, Quilting, and Finishing

CHAPTER
3

Quilting is the "cat's meow" for your appliquéd designs. The lines of stitches create shadows and highlights that add depth and interest to the backgrounds. When used sparingly, quilting can add dimension and definition to the appliquéd cats. I usually slip the needle under the appliquéd pieces, travel between the layers, and come up on the other side to continue the quilted design line.

I prefer random quilting patterns, allowing one quilt design to lead me to the next element. Essentially, a secondary layer of design is formed to complement and complete the picture.

BORDERS

Borders show off your appliquéd picture just as a frame shows off a watercolor or oil painting. You may add one or more borders in various widths. Always measure your finished appliquéd piece and trim to the desired size before adding borders. Be sure the borders opposite each other are the same length. Check also that any unfinished edges of appliqué on the perimeter of the background are caught in the stitching when you add the border. I use a ¼"-wide seam, and sew the side borders first, then the top and bottom. If you add a second border, simply repeat the order.

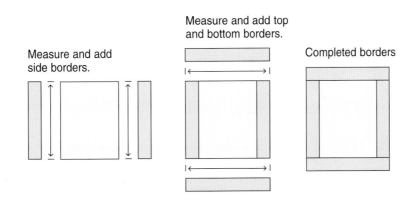

Measure and add side borders.

Measure and add top and bottom borders.

Completed borders

MARKING

When quilting, I mark as little as possible. The less marking I do, the less I have to remove. The amount of marking you'll need depends on the type of design and your level of experience. For consistency, designs that repeat symmetrically should be premarked. A random or free design can be "eyeballed" or marked with your needle as you sew. Drag the needle across the fabric to create a line that will stay just long enough to quilt. In other words, mark as you go.

Use a water-soluble marker and a lightbox to trace the quilting design before the layers are basted. The marking pen may also be used to lightly sketch random patterns after the layers are basted. Masking tape comes in many widths and is handy for marking straight lines. (Do not leave tape on the fabric for any extended period of time.) You can also cut templates in any shape from a non-woven fabric or stiff paper, pin them to the quilt, and stitch around them. The more you quilt, the less you will need to mark.

QUILTING DESIGNS

Ready to quilt, but not sure *what* to quilt? Some element or shape in the appliqué, such as grass or curving branches, may inspire you. Perhaps you want to draw the eye straight to an element of the design—the cat, for example. Begin quilting a design that surrounds the cat, such as echo lines or shells, and work outward. You can add any designs you like in the quilting: heat waves on a sunny afternoon, clouds, or the path of a butterfly's flight. Another idea is to use simple texture designs, such as crosshatching or parallel lines.

Let your imagination be your guide. Jot down possible ideas on paper and start a quilt design file. A few ideas to help you get started are on pages 24-25.

BASTING THE LAYERS

This important step helps keep your quilt smooth and flat during and after quilting. Cut the batting and backing 1" (or more) larger than the top on all sides. Lay out the backing right side down on a smooth, hard surface that will not be harmed by a needle (a cutting mat is great, a dining room table is risky). Add the batting, and finally the quilt top with the right side up. Keep the layers smooth and flat. Using white thread, baste a grid of horizontal and vertical lines about 4" apart using 1"-long stitches. The basted grid keeps everything in place as you quilt.

Basting

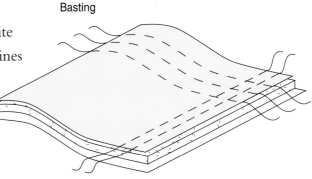

GETTING STARTED WITH QUILTING

I quilt in my lap without a frame; I find this method works best for me. I use a simple running stitch for quilting, and take several stitches on the needle each time.

To begin, knot a 12" to 18"-length of quilting thread. (Too long a piece will fray before you use it all.) Pull the knot through the top into the batting and come up to the top again. Trust the basting and do not push or pull the layers as you quilt. Allow the quilt to relax as you sew. Be sure to catch all three layers. To end a thread, knot the thread close to the quilt top, and pull it into the batting. Let the needle travel between the layers an inch or so, then come up with the needle and snip the thread. This will leave a secure tail inside the quilt.

Quilting stitch

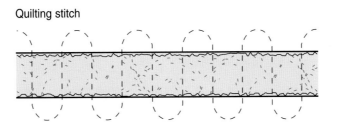

BORDERLESS QUILTS

You can finish off many appliqué designs without borders; just binding. After the appliqué and embroidery are complete, press the top. Do not trim, but if you wish, you can use a water-soluble marker to mark the outside line for the approximate finished size. (Remember, the quilt will shrink a bit after quilting.) Keep the marked piece square. Note if any design elements have raw edges that need to be caught in the binding.

Baste as usual and quilt to the marked edge. Using a rotary cutter, ruler, and mat, trim the quilted piece to size. Once the piece is quilted, you may need to make adjustments to the size to keep the piece square. If you cut through any quilting stitches, machine-stitch about ¼" in from the edge of the quilt before binding. Be careful not to stretch the edges as you sew.

BINDING

Binding is the finishing touch for your quilt. I use a straight, single-fold, cross-grain binding. To make this binding, cut 2"-wide binding strips from selvage to selvage, using a rotary cutter, ruler, and mat. The binding strips are sewn onto the quilt in the same order as the borders: first the sides, then top and bottom. Stitch the binding to the quilt top using a ½" seam allowance. This results in a ½"-wide finished bound edge.

Turn the binding to the back and fold under the raw edge ½". Miter the corners following the illustration. Pin the entire binding in place before stitching it down on the back. Blind stitch it down, being careful not to let any of your stitches go through to the front, and of course, always sign and date your quilt.

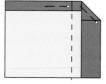

Stitch side binding strip onto quilt.

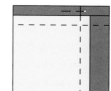

Stitch top binding onto quilt.

Fold as shown.

Fold again as shown.

Fold side strip at a 45° angle.

Fold as shown.

Fold again as shown.

Front

Projects

CHAPTER 4

DESIGNING YOUR OWN PATTERNS

Here are some projects to get you started. Various eye construction techniques and complete instructions for appliqué order are included. Create the projects as they are, or add or subtract design elements as you like. There are sixteen cats and twelve garden flowers.

Feel free to change any of the elements in the various projects. Mix the flowers, make them taller or shorter, bend a stem, or reverse the image. The cats can be moved, too; turn a head, reverse the image, close the eyes, curl a tail, and of course, choose the colors that best represent your favorite feline.

It is fun to play with possible designs. Use white paper, pencil, eraser, and the lightbox for tracing. Begin with the original patterns as a base. You can put more flowers in front or behind the cats. Cover more of the background with appliqué, or design a more open area for your special quilt designs. There are no limits.

Note the watercolors throughout the book. They repeat some of the elements of the projects, as well as provide some new flowers and cats for inspiration. Enlarge them to make your own designs. Once you begin drawing, you will have pages of projects ready to try.

A WORD ABOUT CATS

Most of my appliquéd cats are domestic kitties; that is, non-pedigreed. Seven groups of cats are recognized by cat fanciers: two longhairs (Persian and non-Persian), three shorthaired groups (British and American shorthairs, Oriental shorthairs, and others), plus Siamese and Burmese. All come in a wide range of colors and patterns. Choose the colors you like for your appliquéd cats, take a look at your own (or a friend's) cat for inspiration, or check out a book on cat breeds and expand your knowledge of cat types and temperaments.

Ralph and Simba

Finished size: art area 7" x 8"

MATERIALS

- ⅓ yard muslin for background
- Selection of fabrics for appliqué
- Threads to match appliqué fabrics
- Embroidery floss: tan, brown
- Faux suede: brown, orange, blue
- Permanent markers: black, blue, metallic gold
- White fabric paint
- Fabric glue
- Mats: 10" wide x 11" high; opening: 7" wide x 8" high
- Spray starch

CUTTING

Background: Cut the muslin 12" x 13" for each portrait. It will be trimmed later.

APPLIQUÉ

Appliqué each cat following the numbered order on the pattern. Pre-appliqué the ears for both cats. Appliqué the nose first, and add nostrils later with embroidery. Do the same with the chin and mouth on Simba. The eyes are added last.

This pair is as pretty as a picture, so go ahead and mat and frame these cat portraits. The faces of a Siamese and a Persian are captured in this appliqué-only project.

Ralph

Simba

DETAILS

Ralph

With a single strand of tan floss, stem-stitch the whiskers and eyebrows and add the muzzle dots. Use brown floss in long straight stitches for the ear fur. Add brown satin stitch nostrils. Remove any markings. Press.

EYES: Cut the full eye shapes from brown faux suede. Cut the irises from orange faux suede. Using a permanent black marker, color the edges of the full eye shapes and the pupils. Allow the marker to dry, noting that marker is slow to dry on faux suede. Add some blue lines to the irises in permanent marker. Add a metallic gold outline to the pupils and a few gold dots to the orange irises. Add white pupil highlights with fabric paint. Glue the irises to the full eye shapes. Glue the finished eyes to the appliquéd cat. Allow the glue to dry.

Simba

With a single strand of tan floss, stem-stitch the whiskers. Satin-stitch the nostrils and mouth in brown. Use long straight stitches in tan for the ear fur.

EYES: Cut the full eye shapes from brown faux suede. Cut the irises from blue faux suede. Using a permanent black marker, color the edges of the full eye shapes and the pupils. Allow the marker to dry, noting that marker is slow to dry on faux suede. Add some blue lines to the irises. Add white highlights to the pupils with fabric paint. Glue the irises to the full eye shapes. Glue the finished eyes to the appliquéd cat. Allow the glue to dry. (Optional: I used a brown stem stitch to outline the eyes.)

Remove any markings. Press each portrait from the back using several applications of spray starch. A bit of pressing on the front of the appliqué may be necessary. Trim to a shy 10" wide x 11" high. Mat and frame the portraits.

RALPH

Enlarge 205%.

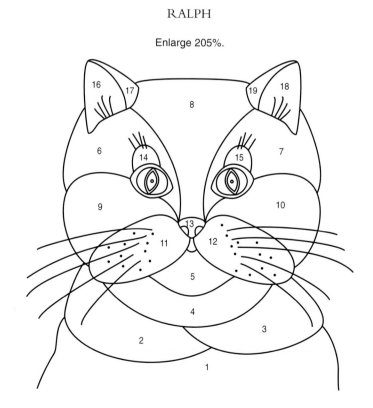

SIMBA

Enlarge 205%.

Ezra and Leaves

Finished size: 20" x 24"

MATERIALS

- 1 yard muslin for background and backing
- Selection of fabrics for appliqué
- ¼ yard red fabric for binding
- Batting: 22" x 26"
- Threads to match appliqué fabrics
- Natural-color quilting thread
- Embroidery floss: gray, white

CUTTING

Background: Cut the muslin 22" x 26". It will be trimmed later.
Binding: Cut four 2"-wide strips selvage to selvage.

APPLIQUÉ

Begin with the blades of grass behind the cat (1 through 4). Pre-appliqué the two-piece blade 2 onto 1. Appliqué stems 1–3. Butt up the end of stem 3 to the appliquéd edge of stem 2. Add leaves 4–10. The rest of the leaves can be added any time, except 11 is added after the cat is appliquéd.

Begin the cat with 1, the ear. Pre-appliqué 6 onto 5. Appliqué the eye pieces. See detail.

Pre-appliqué 10 onto 9. Pre-appliqué the forward ear, 13 onto 12, add 14, then 15. Appliqué the pre-appliquéd ear to the background. Pre-appliqué 20 onto 19. After the cat is finished, appliqué the grasses. I have numbered them from the left to the right starting with 1. Pre-appliqué the two-piece blades, the higher number over the lower number.

"No one can see me here." A tan cat sits motionless behind the red-stemmed foliage and bright green blades of grass. The quilting highlights the cat and gives serenity to the piece.

DETAILS

Add a few stitches of white to the pupil for a highlight. Stem-stitch the mouth in gray. With a single strand of gray, stem-stitch the whiskers and add the muzzle dots. Remove any markings. Press and baste for quilting.

QUILTING

This one is simple but has a great look. Quilt a halo encompassing the head and shoulder of the cat. Radiate lines inside the circle. Echo the circle outward, starting ½" out and increasing the distance between echo lines as you go outward. Add some quilting around some of the cat pieces and in any area of the cat you like.

Trim the piece to approximately 20" wide x 24" high. Bind, measuring the piece for the exact length of binding strips before you stitch (see page 26).

PATTERN FOR EZRA AND THE LEAVES

Enlarge 267%.

11 after cat

Meesta and Sunflowers

Finished size: 20" x 25"

MATERIALS

- 1 yard muslin for background and backing
- Selection of fabrics for appliqué
- ¼ yard black fabric for binding
- Batting: 22" x 27"
- Threads to match appliqué fabrics
- Natural-color quilting thread
- Black permanent marker

CUTTING

Background: Cut the muslin 22" x 27". It will be trimmed later.

Binding: Cut three 2"-wide strips selvage to selvage.

APPLIQUÉ

Begin with the cat, starting with 1, the tail. Pre-appliqué 2 onto 1, 6 onto 5, and 8 onto 7. Pre-appliqué the left ear part 15 onto 14, then add 16. Number 17 is the eyes.

First appliqué the white underlayer. There are no turned-under edges, so baste each whole white piece on the marked spot on the background. Pre-appliqué the eyeballs.

Cat's paws step cautiously along the pebbled path lined with glorious sunflowers left and right. The radiating lines of quilting draw the eye to the center star: the cat.

For each eye, cut the entire eye shape (with allowance) from black, marking the placement of the iris. Appliqué the iris on top of the black, using the whole shape, including the pupil. Embroider the pupil on top of the iris in black satin stitch. Stitch the completed eye in place on the white background, leaving some white showing as you appliqué. Patience is the key with these small parts.

Pre-appliqué 19 onto 18. Be sure to turn under and stitch the edges of 18 that meet the white of the eye. You may appliqué the nose, 34, onto the black nostrils or color the nostrils later, treating the nose and nostrils as one piece. Using the tiny bias technique (see page 17), appliqué all the leaf stems, followed by the main flower stems. There are two versions of the blossom, A and B. Follow the order of appliqué for each as marked. For the leaves, first pre-appliqué 2 onto 1.

DETAILS

With black permanent marker, color nostrils (unless you appliquéd the color). I used silver-gray floss in long straight stitches for the ear fur. Use this same sparkle in a stem stitch around the white of the eye. Add a few white stitches to the pupil of each eye. Stem-stitch the toe lines in black. With a single strand of black, add the muzzle dots and stem-stitch the whiskers. Remove any markings and press. Baste for quilting.

QUILTING

Begin with diagonal lines from the top of each cat leg to the lower corners. Make the lines a bit wavy and echo once. Fill in the center area with random pebble shapes. Radiate lines outward from the cat body to the edges.

Remove basting and trim to approximately 20" x 25". Bind, measuring the piece for the exact length of binding strips before you stitch (see page 26).

PATTERN FOR MEESTA
AND SUNFLOWERS

Enlarge 216%.

37

Fred in the Rudbeckia

Finished size: 19" x 25"

MATERIALS

- 1 yard muslin for background and backing
- Selection of fabrics for appliqué
- ¼ yard green fabric for binding
- Batting: 21" x 27"
- Threads to match appliqué fabrics
- Natural-color quilting thread
- Embroidery floss: gray, beige, dark brown
- Black permanent marker

CUTTING

Background: Cut the muslin 21" x 27". It will be trimmed later.

Binding: Cut four 2"-wide strips selvage to selvage.

A bright, sun-warmed rock sends this cat into dreamland. Black-eyed Susans rimmed with gold stand guard over our purring sleeper. Sun and warmth are there in the quilted design.

APPLIQUÉ

Begin with the rock: two pieces that may be appliquéd top over bottom or bottom over top. Follow by appliquéing the three top flowers, stems first (they are all flower A). Follow the numbered order for the flowers and add the leaves.

Begin the cat body at 1. Pre-appliqué 9 onto 8. Pre-appliqué the right ear, 10 onto 11, 11 onto 12. Add the toes and foot pads any time. Treat the chin and mouth, 22, as one. The mouth will be added later. Treat the nose and nostrils, 25, as one piece also. Pre-appliqué the left ear, 26 onto 27, 27 onto 28. Add to the background. Appliqué the rest of the flowers. Starting with the stems, use the tiny bias technique (see page 17). Add the leaves. There are two styles of flowers on the rock: B and C. Follow the numbered order for each.

DETAILS

Using gray embroidery floss, use single straight stitches for the ear fur. Use dark brown and a satin stitch for the eyes and mouth. Use a dark brown stem stitch for the line below the nose. With a single strand of beige, stem-stitch the whiskers and add the muzzle dots. In beige, use single, long straight stitches for the eyebrows. Darken the nostrils with a permanent marker. Remove any markings. Press and baste for quilting.

QUILTING

Begin in the upper-left corner with the sun. Radiate circles out in echo lines about ¼" apart for 3" to 4". Echo out again 1¼". Fill in this space with zigzagging lines or simple stars. Add the long, triangular sunrays. Stitch lazy, back-and-forth loops upward from the rock and cat for heat waves. Echo the line of the feet and rock to fill in the lower right background. Fill in the remaining upper spaces with asterisk-style stars. Quilt around the flowers and the cat as you like. Fill in any large areas of the cat as desired.

Remove basting. Trim the piece to approximately 19" x 25". Bind, measuring the piece for the exact length of binding strips before you stitch (see page 26).

PATTERN FOR FRED IN THE RUDBECKIA

Enlarge 120%.

Jake Prowling in the Salvia

Finished size: 21" x 15"

MATERIALS

- ½ yard muslin for background and backing
- Selection of fabrics for appliqué
- ¼ yard red fabric for border
- ¼ yard green fabric for binding
- Batting: 23" x 17"
- Threads to match appliqué fabrics
- Natural-color quilting thread

CUTTING

Background: Cut the muslin 21" x 15". It will be trimmed later.

Border: Cut two 2¼"-wide strips selvage to selvage.

Binding: Cut four 2"-wide strips selvage to selvage.

A simple silhouetted cat prowls among the scarlet salvia. Quilted, starlit skies fill the background of this peek at a nocturnal kitty.

APPLIQUÉ

Begin with the stems and leaves behind the silhouette, starting at 1 at the top of the cat's back, and working through piece 5. Appliqué the cat silhouette, 6. (This large piece can be pinned or basted in place on the background.) Clip the curves as you stitch (see Inside Curves, page 16). Appliqué the remaining stems using the tiny bias technique (see page 17). Add the leaves. Note when one leaf overlaps another in the lower right; appliqué the underneath leaf first. Add the salvia flowers. Some of these petals overlap also; stitch the underneath petals first.

Remove any markings. Press and trim the background to 18½" x 12½". Add borders, measuring the piece for the exact length of borders before you stitch (see page 21). Baste for quilting.

QUILTING

Quilt around the cat and echo-quilt once about ¼" from the first stitching. Surround the cat with large loops. Echo the outside line of the loops with three lines about ¼" apart. Radiate lines from the approximate center of each loop area. At the bottom, continue the ¼" echo lines to the edge. At the top, create sections of radiating lines at random.

Remove basting and trim to approximately 21" x 15". Bind, measuring the piece for the exact length of binding strips before you stitch (see page 26).

PATTERN FOR JAKE
PROWLING IN THE SALVIA

Enlarge 173%.

6

5

Niko and Hydrangea

Finished size: 15" x 11"

MATERIALS

- ½ yard muslin for background and backing
- Selection of fabrics for appliqué
- ⅛ yard black fabric for binding
- Batting: 17" x 13"
- Threads to match appliqué fabrics
- Natural-color quilting thread
- Embroidery floss: dark brown, white, tan, black, yellow, gray, green
- White faux suede for eyes
- Black permanent marker
- Fabric paint: green, white
- Fabric glue

CUTTING

Background: Cut the muslin 17" x 13". It will be trimmed later.

Binding: Cut two 2"-wide strips selvage to selvage.

APPLIQUÉ

Begin the cat with the tail, 1. Use the tiny bias technique for stems 3 and 4 (see page 17). Pre-appliqué 6 onto 5. Leave an opening on the foot, 5, to slip the stem under; appliqué the opening after the stem is in place. Treat the mouth and chin, 12, as one piece and add the mouth later. Pre-appliqué 14 onto 13, then 16 onto 15. Stitch the ears to the background. Treat the nose and nostrils, 22, as one piece. Nostrils will be added later.

> "See, the leaves match my eyes." A self-assured cat poses with his favorite cherry-pink hydrangea bloom. The quilting is designed to show off the kitty.

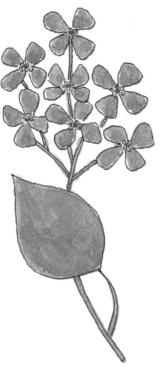

Use the tiny bias technique for the stems (see page 17). Add the leaves. You may follow the numbered order 1–29 for the flower petals or use any order, as the overlap pattern is not critical. Note that the petals do not touch in the center of each flower.

DETAILS

Cluster white French knots at the center of each floret. Add one yellow and one black French knot to the center of the cluster of white knots. Use green to make two parallel rows of stem stitch for the stems leading to the florets. With dark brown stem stitch, define the toes and the line below the nose. In the same dark brown, use satin stitch to add the mouth and nostrils. With gray, add the ear fur in straight stitches. With a single strand of tan, stem-stitch the eyebrows, whiskers, and muzzle dots. Remove any markings and press.

EYES: Cut the eye shapes from white faux suede. Using a black permanent marker or paint, color the pupil and edges of the eye. Color the iris green using your fabric paint (a blend of several greens will give more dimension). Add a white highlight to the pupil with paint. After the eyes are completely dry, glue them to the cat. Allow the glue to dry thoroughly before handling the background. With a white stem stitch, outline each eye. Baste for quilting.

QUILTING

Begin with the partial halo that circles the cat. Use a large plate or other round object for a pattern. Echo-quilt the circle once, approximately ¼" out. Add lines of echo quilting around the appliqués at the bottom until you reach the edge of the quilt. Radiate lines inside the circle more or less from the center. Add a round of teardrops around the outside of the circle. Fill in the remaining area with echo lines, ¼" or so apart. Remove any basting. Trim the piece to approximately 15" x 11". Bind, measuring the piece for the exact length of binding strips before you stitch (see page 26).

PATTERN FOR
NIKO AND
HYDRANGEA

Enlarge 219%.

27 - all leaf stems

Rosie, Queen of the Roses

Finished size: 16½" x 21½"

MATERIALS

- ⅔ yard muslin for background and backing
- Selection of fabrics for appliqué
- ¼ yard pink fabric for border
- ¼ yard tan fabric for binding
- Batting: 20" x 25"
- Threads to match the appliqué fabrics
- Natural-color quilting thread
- Embroidery floss: black, tan
- Faux suede: black, green
- Fabric paint: white to dot the eye
- Black permanent marker
- Fabric glue

CUTTING

Background: Cut the muslin 15" x 21". It will be trimmed later.

Borders: Cut two 2½"-wide strips selvage to selvage.

Binding: Cut three 2"-wide strips selvage to selvage.

APPLIQUÉ

Using the tiny bias technique (see page 17), appliqué the bud stems numbered 1, followed by the two main upper stems numbered 2.

Begin the cat with the tail, 1, and follow the numbered order of appliqué. Note 7A and 7B are the rose stems. On the chin, 12, include the dark mouth as part of the whole piece and embroider the dark color later. For the right ear, pre-appliqué 16 onto 15. Sew this to 14, add 17, and appliqué the pre-assembled ear to the background. For the left ear, pre-appliqué 19 onto 18; add 20, then 21. Appliqué the pre-assembled ear to the background.

Pretty as a princess, a pampered pet rests among her bouquet of long-stemmed roses. Varied quilting designs grow outward from Her Highness.

Pre-appliqué 23 onto 22, 25 onto 24, and add to the background. Note that 30 and 31 are the full piece of white. The eye will be on top of this white. Treat the nose and nostrils, 33, as one piece. The nostrils will be defined later.

Appliqué the rosebuds and roses according to the numbered order for each. Add the leaves.

EYES

From faux suede, cut the back pieces from black and the iris from green. Treat each as a whole piece. That is; the black back includes the iris, the iris includes the pupil. Glue the irises to the black backgrounds. Color the pupils with a permanent black marker. Dot each pupil with a white fabric paint highlight. Set the eyes aside to dry.

DETAILS

With a single strand of black floss, add the whiskers using a stem stitch. Add tiny single stitches for the muzzle dots. Satin-stitch the mouth in black. Use long, tan straight stitches for the ear fur. With a permanent black marker, carefully color the nostrils. With a tan stem stitch, add the lines that separate the toes.

Remove any markings. Press and trim the background to 13" x 18½". Glue the eyes on. Allow the glue to dry completely before handling the background. Add the borders, measuring the piece for the exact length of the borders before you stitch (see page 21). Baste for quilting.

QUILTING

Quilt around the cat and as many cat pieces as you like for definition. You can also add quilting to the cat itself. Quilt radiating triangles around the cat; on the right side I stitched two rows. Connect the triangle tops with arched lines. Echo each line twice. Add random shells around three rows. Finish the bottom half in shells, continuing right through the borders. At the top, add another row of radiating triangles, again connecting the triangle tops with arched and double-echoed lines. Continue to the top with random shells.

Remove basting and trim to approximately 16½" x 21½". Bind, measuring the piece for the exact length of binding strips before you stitch (see page 26).

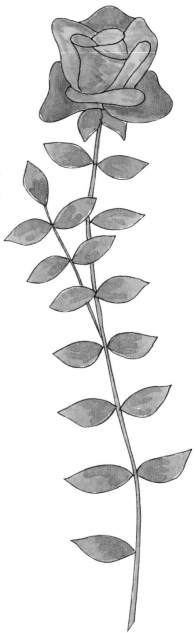

PATTERN FOR ROSIE,
QUEEN OF THE ROSES

Enlarge 162%.

Snowball in the Irises

Finished size: 19" x 24"

MATERIALS

- 1 yard muslin for background and backing
- Selection of fabrics for appliqué
- ¼ yard purple fabric for binding
- Batting: 22" x 27"
- Threads to match the appliqué fabrics
- Natural-color quilting thread
- Embroidery floss: gray, black, blue, white, yellow

CUTTING

Background: Cut the muslin 22" x 27". It will be trimmed later.

Binding: Cut three 2"-wide strips selvage to selvage.

APPLIQUÉ

First appliqué four pieces of the flowers, 1A–4A. These are the lower stem and leaf that come from behind the cat, and the two-part leaf behind the left ear.

Begin the cat with 1, the space between the front legs. Baste this piece in place, as it has no turn-under. Keep the basting within the allowance. Continue following the numbered order of the cat. Pre-appliqué both ears: 14 onto 13 and add 15, 17 onto 16 and add 18. Stitch both ear units onto the background. Treat the mouth and chin, 25, as one piece. The mouth will be colored later. Treat the nose and nostrils, 28, as one piece. The nostrils will be colored later.

A soft-furred white cat owns this iris bed. Deep purple complements the blue-green of the long leaves. A crisp-lined quilting pattern broken by feathered plumes is as elegant as the regal flowers and proud creature.

Appliqué the irises, following the numbered pieces. Begin with the upper leaf on the left, 1, through leaf pieces 5 and 6. Pre-appliqué all two-part leaves. Continue with stems 7-18. Add leaves 19-28, then stems 29 and 30. Appliqué the three-piece buds, numbered 1-3. There are two flower shapes, A and B. On all, pre-appliqué 2 onto 1, 6 onto 5, 10 onto 9, and 12 onto 11.

DETAILS

On the flowers, use yellow straight stitches that radiate from the center downward. Add a white French knot to each flower center. The eyes are embroidered. Using a stem stitch, outline the eyes in black. Satin-stitch the iris in blue and fill in the remaining areas with black satin stitch. Add a few white stitches to the pupils for highlights. With gray floss and satin stitch, fill in the mouth and nostrils. With a single strand of floss, stem-stitch the whiskers in gray and add the muzzle dots. Stem-stitch the toe lines in gray and the eyebrows in white. Use white straight stitches for the ear fur. Remove any markings. Press and baste for quilting.

QUILTING

Begin with the two curved feathers. No two feathers ever come out the same. Quilt the two-line center vein first and add the feathers working down from the top. Fill in the rest of the background with random lines, leaving ¾" spaces between lines, and changing direction at will. Quilt around the cat and your choice of flowers and cat pieces. Add quilting to the cat itself if you like.

Remove basting and trim the piece to approximately 19½ " x 24½". Bind, measuring the piece for the exact length of binding strips before you stitch (see page 26).

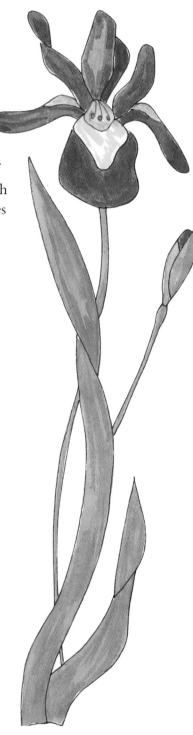

PATTERN FOR SNOWBALL
IN THE IRISES

Enlarge 245%.

Molly, Sassy, and the Tulips

Finished size: 22" x 16¼"

MATERIALS

- ⅔ yard muslin for background and backing
- Selection of fabrics for appliqué
- ¼ yard green for border
- ¼ yard black for the binding
- Batting: 24" x 19"
- Threads to match appliqué fabrics
- Natural-color quilting thread
- Embroidery floss: gray, black, tan
- Faux suede: greens, blue
- Black permanent marker
- White fabric pen to dot the eyes
- Fabric glue

CUTTING

Background: Cut the muslin 2l" x 16". It will be trimmed later.

Borders: Cut three 2½"-wide strips selvage to selvage.

Binding: Cut three 2"-wide strips selvage to selvage.

APPLIQUÉ

The right-hand cat, the kitten, is first. Follow the numbered order of appliqué beginning with the neck, 1. Pre-appliqué 4 onto 3 to construct the ear. Sew the ear to the background. For 7, ignore the eye and cut as a solid piece. Treat the nose and nostrils, 11, as one piece. Pre-appliqué 14 onto 13 and 15 over 14. Appliqué this ear unit to the background. Add the eye background in black as a whole piece, including the iris and pupil.

This mother and child duo is sweet together in a patch of bright red tulips. Simple scattered hearts amplify the message, and traditional crosshatch quilting gives a warm and cozy nostalgic feeling.

The left-hand cat is second. Follow the numbered order of appliqué with the body, 1. Pre-appliqué the ear pieces, 4 onto 3, and stitch the ear to the background. Pre-appliqué 6 onto 5. Note piece 7 is the complete size with piece 8 sewn on top. Treat the nose and nostril, 13, as one. The nostril will be added later. Treat the eye background as a solid piece as with the kitten's eye.

Follow the appliqué order for the tulips beginning with the left stem, 1. Pre-appliqué 21 onto 20. Also pre-appliqué 28 onto 27 and 30 onto 29.

EYES

Cut a green faux suede iris for the left cat and a blue iris for the kitten. With a black permanent marker, color the pupils, and add a white highlight to each with white paint.

DETAILS

With a single strand of gray, stem-stitch the whiskers and muzzle dots. With a single strand of tan, add the ear fur with long straight stitches.

Use a single gray strand for the eyebrows with a stem stitch. Black satin stitching creates nostrils on each cat's nose. With a single strand of black and a stem stitch, outline the mouth.

Remove any markings. Press and trim the background to 19" x 13½". Glue the irises onto the eyes and allow the glue to dry. Add the borders, measuring for the exact length of the borders before you stitch (see page 21). Be sure to catch the side of the left cat and the bottoms of both cats in the border seam. Baste for quilting.

QUILTING

Begin with the scattered hearts. Quilting around a template of stiff interfacing works well. Double the outline of the hearts and fill the interior with random shells. Crosshatch the entire background and border at a 45° angle, using ¾"-wide masking tape as a guide. Quilt around the leaves, flowers, and cat pieces as you like. You may also add quilting to the cats if you choose.

Remove basting and trim the outer edge to approximately 22" x 16¼". Bind, measuring the piece for the exact length of binding strips before you stitch (see page 26).

PATTERN FOR MOLLY, SASSY, AND THE TULIPS

Enlarge 232%.

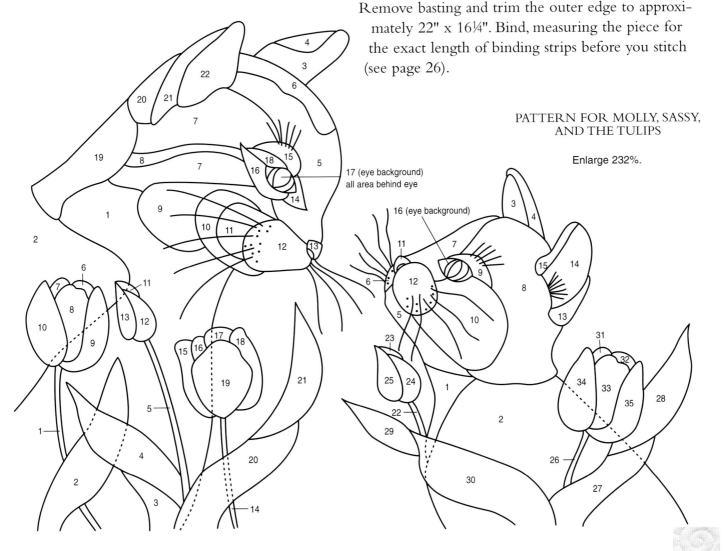

Ollie Playing in the Pansies

Finished size: 22" x 16½"

MATERIALS

- ¾ yard muslin for background and backing
- Selection of fabrics for appliqué
- ¼ yard pink fabric for border
- ¼ yard green fabric for binding
- Batting: 24" x 19"
- Threads to match the appliqué fabrics
- Natural-color quilting thread
- Embroidery floss: white, black, brown
- Black permanent marker
- Fabric paint: blue, white

CUTTING

Background: Cut the muslin 21" x 15". It will be trimmed later.
Borders: Cut three 2½"-wide strips.
Binding: Cut three 2"-wide strips selvage to selvage.

APPLIQUÉ

Begin with the cat's tummy, 1. After piece 3, appliqué the rock. Be sure to mark the placement lines for the flowers and leaves on the rock. Leave an opening on the right side (marked in pink) for slipping the stem in. Stitch down after the stem is appliquéd. Treat the chin and mouth, 10, as one piece. The mouth will be added later. Treat the nose and nostrils, 16, as one piece. The nostrils will be added later. Cut the eyes, 22, from black fabric. Cut the whole eye shape with a turn-under allowance.

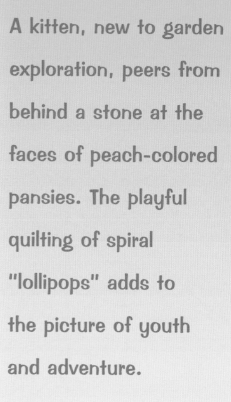

A kitten, new to garden exploration, peers from behind a stone at the faces of peach-colored pansies. The playful quilting of spiral "lollipops" adds to the picture of youth and adventure.

With blue fabric paint, color the iris and add the white highlight dot to the pupil on both eyes. Allow the paint to dry. Press the eyes and appliqué the edges that will be exposed to the background. Pre-appliqué the left ear, 28 onto 27, add 29, then 30. Stitch the ear to the background. Pre-appliqué the right ear, 32 onto 31, add 33, then 34. Stitch the ear to the background.

Begin the stems and leaves with stem 1 on the left. Note the stems of the leaves are cut in a single piece along with the leaves. Cut so the stem runs on the bias. Use the tiny bias technique (see page 17) for the stems. After adding the stem, 3, stitch down the rest of the rock. Pre-appliqué any two-piece leaves, the higher number onto the lower. Keep leaves 13 and 20 free on the part that covers the blossoms; appliqué them down after the blossoms are in place. Appliqué the blossoms according to their individual numbered order. On the A blossoms, pre-appliqué 4 onto 3, 6 onto 5, and 8 onto 7.

DETAILS

Make long, white straight stitches out of the centers of blossoms A, and add a black French knot to each center. With white straight stitches, add the ear fur. Satin-stitch the mouth in brown. With a single brown strand, stem-stitch the whiskers and add the muzzle dots. Stem-stitch the toe lines in brown. Use a black permanent marker to darken the nostrils.

Remove any markings. Press. Trim to 19" x 13". Be sure to cut the bottom first so the raw edges of the rock and the stems are included in the border seam. Add borders, measuring the piece for the exact length of borders before you stitch (see page 21). Press. Baste for quilting.

PATTERN FOR OLLIE
PLAYING IN THE PANSIES

Enlarge 143%.

QUILTING

Begin with the scattered spiral "lollipops." Next, using ¾"-wide masking tape, quilt the vertical lines in the muslin background. Quilt the background along the inside of the border. Using ¾"-wide masking tape, quilt the border. Add some shells in the border as shown in the photo. Quilt around any flowers, leaves, and cat pieces you like.

Remove basting and trim to approximately 22" x 16½". Bind, measuring the piece for the exact length of binding strips before you stitch (see page 26).

Sam and the Gladioli

Finished size: 15½" x 27½"

MATERIAL

- 1 yard muslin for background and backing
- Selection of fabrics for appliqué
- ¼ yard red fabric for border
- ¼ yard green fabric for binding
- Batting: 17" x 30"
- Threads to match the appliqué fabrics
- Natural-color quilting thread
- Embroidery floss: gray, black, red, yellow, white
- Faux suede: black, green
- White fabric paint
- Black permanent marker
- Fabric glue

A tall picket, tall gladioli stalks, and a cat reaching up for an escaping butterfly create this charming vertical piece. Straight lines of quilting continue the linear theme.

CUTTING

Background: Cut the muslin 14" x 27". It will be trimmed later.

Borders: Cut three 2"-wide strips selvage to selvage.

Binding: Cut three 2"-wide strips selvage to selvage.

APPLIQUÉ

Appliqué the grass at the bottom (pieces 1 and 2). Leave the bottom and sides raw-edged as these will be caught in the border seam. Pre-appliqué the fence picket 3, 4, and 5, and stitch to the background. Leave the left side raw-edged, as this will be caught in the border seam.

Appliqué the cat following the numbered pattern. Begin with the toe, 1. Leave the tip of the tail, 5, free until the leaf has been added, then appliqué it down on top. Number 11 is simply placed on the background and basted down in the allowance;

it has no turn-under. Make this piece the entire area, including the eye. Pre-appliqué the ear, 16 onto 15 and the edge of 16 onto 14. Stitch the finished ear to the background. Pre-appliqué 18 onto 17 and add to the background. Be sure to clip the curve as you appliqué the edge around the white eye space (see page 16). Treat the nose and nostril as one piece. The nostril will be added later. Appliqué the butterfly wings, 1, 2, and 3. Turn under the allowance all around on 3.

Begin the gladioli with the two-piece buds at the top of each stalk, order of appliqué 1, 2. There are nine buds. Next add the 1, 2, and 3 broad leaves. Using the tiny bias technique (see page 17), add the stems. Note that the stems that begin under others are added first. Stitch the lower leaves beginning with the lower left leaf, 1. Pre-appliqué the two-piece leaves before adding them to the picture. Follow the numbered order for the petals beginning with 11 for the left stalk, 1 for the center stalk, and 1 again for the right stalk. Remember to sew down the tail tip.

EYES

Cut the back eye shape from black faux suede. Cut the iris from green. Glue the iris on top of the black. Color the pupil with a permanent black marker. Use a dot of white fabric paint for the highlight.

DETAILS

Use long straight stitches for the flower stamens in white, with tips of three perpendicular stitches at the ends of the stamens in yellow. Using a single strand of gray floss, embroider the cat's whiskers and add the muzzle dots. Also in gray, add the toe lines with a stem stitch, and ear fur with straight stitches. Add a line of stem stitch at the lip split in gray. Add pairs of French knots in red and yellow to the butterfly wings. Satin-stitch the butterfly body in black. Using a single strand of black, stem-stitch the antennae and legs. Add a few extra stitches to the end of the antennae to form a club shape. With a permanent black marker, add the cat's nostril.

Remove any markings and press. Trim the background to 12" x 25". Glue the eye onto the cat and allow the glue to dry. Add the borders, measuring the piece for the exact length of strips before you stitch (see page 21). Be sure to catch all raw edges of tail, grass, and picket in the seams. Baste for quilting.

QUILTING

Quilt around the cat and along the picket. Fill the muslin background and the border with random lines. A piece of masking tape to guide your quilting is helpful here. Quilt around the background along the inside of the border. Quilt around and within any cat pieces you choose.

Remove basting and trim the outer edge to approximately 15" x 27½". Bind, measuring the piece for the exact length of binding strips before you stitch (see page 26).

PATTERN FOR SAM
AND THE GLADIOLI

Enlarge 293%.

Otis Hangin' in the Wisteria

Finished size: 15½" x 17½"

MATERIAL

- ⅔ yard muslin for background and backing
- Selection of fabrics for appliqué
- ¼ yard green fabric for border
- ¼ yard purple fabric for binding
- Batting: 18" x 20"
- Threads to match appliqué fabrics
- Natural-color quilting thread
- Embroidery floss: white, yellow, beige, gold, tan, green

CUTTING

Background: Cut the muslin 14" x 16". It will be trimmed later.
Borders: Cut two 2½"-wide strips, selvage to selvage.
Binding: Cut two 2"-wide strips, selvage to selvage.

APPLIQUÉ

Begin the appliqué with the cat's tummy, 1. Leave the areas on the branches indicated in pink unappliquéd where the leaf stems will go under. Pre-appliqué 10 onto 8 and 9. Pre-appliqué 13 onto 12. Pre-appliqué both eye pieces. Cut the black background plus turn-under allowance. Stitch on the green iris. Appliqué the pupil on top of the iris. Turn under and appliqué only those edges that will not be covered by another appliqué. Appliqué the pink nose onto black for nostrils, or treat the nose and nostrils as one piece and add the nostrils later in marker or embroidery.

A bit out of reach, the pretty purple blossoms tickle this daring cat who is just "hanging in there." Quilted leaves and intersecting branches continue the viny growth of the wisteria.

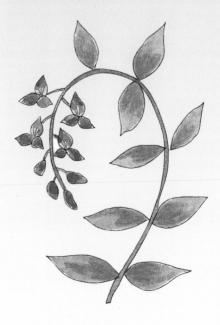

Using the tiny bias technique (see page 17), appliqué the leaf stems, tucking the ends under the branches. Appliqué the openings on the branches. Add the leaves. Stitch the flowers and buds, following the numbered order on each individual flower.

DETAILS

Stem-stitch the eyebrows with a single strand of white floss. Use a few white stitches for the pupil highlights. Use tan straight stitches for the ear fur. Use a single strand of beige and a stem stitch for the whiskers and muzzle dots. Complete the blossoms by making three yellow straight stitches up from the center of each three-petal flower, and one French knot in white. Use a double row of green stem stitch for the main flower stem and a single row for the side stems. Remove any markings. Press. Trim the background to 12" x 14". Add the borders, measuring the piece for the exact length of borders before you stitch (see page 21). Baste for quilting.

QUILTING

Fill the background and border below the horizontal branch with center-veined leaves. Quilt around the cat above the branch and echo twice. Create a grid with wavy, double lines above the branch. I quilted right to the outer edge of the border. Quilt around and in any cat pieces you like. Remove basting and trim to approximately 15½" x 17½". Bind, measuring the piece for the exact length of binding strips before you stitch (see page 26).

Enlarge 235%.

Mocha in the Periwinkle

Finished size: 24½" x 19"

MATERIALS

- 1 yard muslin for background and backing
- Selection of fabrics for appliqué
- ½ yard green fabric for binding
- Batting: 27" x 21"
- Threads to match appliqué fabrics
- Natural-color quilting thread
- Embroidery floss: green, white, rust or orange, black, red, brown, tan

CUTTING

Background: Cut the muslin 27" x 21". It will be trimmed later.

Binding: Cut three 2"-wide strips selvage to selvage.

A curious cat casually plays with bright butterflies amid the viny periwinkle. Grasses in appliqué are multiplied with quilted blades, and the sky fills with the flight paths of winged creatures.

APPLIQUÉ

Begin with the cat tail, 1. Leave the edges of the cat's body unappliquéd so the stems can be slipped under; sew these edges down later. Pre-appliqué 2 onto 3 and 4 onto 2. Appliqué each eye as a solid black piece (18 and 24). The details will be added later. The nose, 27, can be appliquéd onto black nostrils, or the nose and nostrils can be treated as one piece and the nostrils colored in later with permanent marker or embroidery. Pre-appliqué 29 onto 28 and 30 onto 29. Stitch the pre-appliquéd arm and shoulder to the background. Pre-appliqué 32 onto 31. Add these to the cat to finish.

PATTERN FOR MOCHA
IN THE PERIWINKLE

Enlarge 217%.

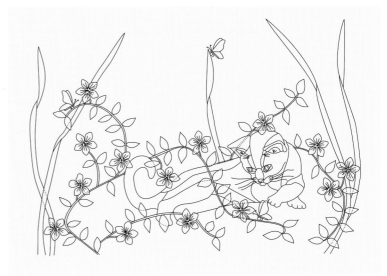

Add the grasses, starting with the blade farthest to the right. Pre-appliqué each two-piece blade, 2 onto 1. Add the periwinkle stems using the tiny bias technique (see page 17). Begin with all the small flower stems. Remember to stitch down the areas left open earlier. Add the leaves, flower petals, and the butterflies. Turn under the lower wing where it meets the body. This will give a smooth edge for embroidery.

DETAILS

Using a satin stitch, embroider the irises of the eyes in green. Add a white stitch to the pupil area for a highlight and a white stem stitch around the eye itself. Use straight stitches in white for the eyebrows and two strands of floss and a stem stitch for the whiskers. Add a mouth in black stem stitch if you like. A group of tan straight stitches adds the ear fur. Brown stem stitching draws the toe lines. The periwinkle blooms have white straight stitches from the petals to the open center, two or so per petal. Add a rust or orange French knot to each flower center. Satin-stitch the butterfly bodies and heads in brown. Use a single strand of brown floss to stem stitch the antennae and legs. Add a French knot to the end of each antenna. I added a row of red French knots on the upper wing of each butterfly. Remove any markings. Press and baste for quilting.

QUILTING

I began with random blades of grass of varying heights from the bottom of the quilt. The remaining sky was filled with large looped lines. Quilt around or in any cat pieces you like.

Remove basting and trim the quilt to approximately 25" x 19". Bind, measuring the piece for the exact length of binding strips before you stitch (see page 26).

Opie in the Sunshine

Finished size: 19" x 13" or 15" x 10½"

MATERIALS

Quilted Cat

19" x 13"

- ½ yard muslin for background and backing
- ¼ yard fabric of your choice for binding
- Batting: 22" x 16"
- Natural-color and dark brown quilting thread
- Pigma pens: black, brown, blue

Embroidered Cat

19" x 13"

- ½ yard muslin for background and backing
- ¼ yard fabric of your choice for binding
- Batting: 22" x 16"
- Natural-color and dark brown quilting thread
- Embroidery floss: green, white, pink, black

Painted Cat

15" x 10½"

- ½ yard muslin for background and backing
- ¼ yard fabric of your choice for binding
- Batting: 18" x 13"
- Natural-color and dark brown quilting thread
- Pigma pen: black
- Fabric paints: titanium white, cerulean blue, cadmium red, raw umber, yellow oxide

There is more than one way to stitch a cat! How about a quilted cat, an embroidered cat, or even a painted cat? I offer three cats, each created using a different technique. Lots of possibilities, lots of fun!

 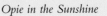

CUTTING

Quilted Cat

Background: Cut the muslin 20" x 14". It will be trimmed later.

Binding: Cut two 2"-wide strips selvage to selvage.

Embroidered Cat

Background: Cut the muslin 20" x 14". It will be trimmed later.

Binding: Cut two 2"-wide strips selvage to selvage.

Painted Cat

Background: Cut the muslin 16" x 11½". It will be trimmed later.

Binding: Cut two 2"-wide strips selvage to selvage.

DIRECTIONS

Quilted Cat

Trace the cat design onto the background fabric using a removable marker. Baste for quilting.

DETAILS

Stitch the cat as drawn with dark brown quilting thread. Use the Pigma pens to color the eyes, nose, mouth, whiskers, and muzzle dots.

QUILTING

The remaining quilting is done with natural-color thread. Stitch random lines inside the cat. Echo around the cat, then downward. Radiate lines upward from the cat.

Remove markings and basting, and trim the quilt to approximately 19" x 13". Bind, measuring the piece for the exact length of binding strips before you stitch (see page 26).

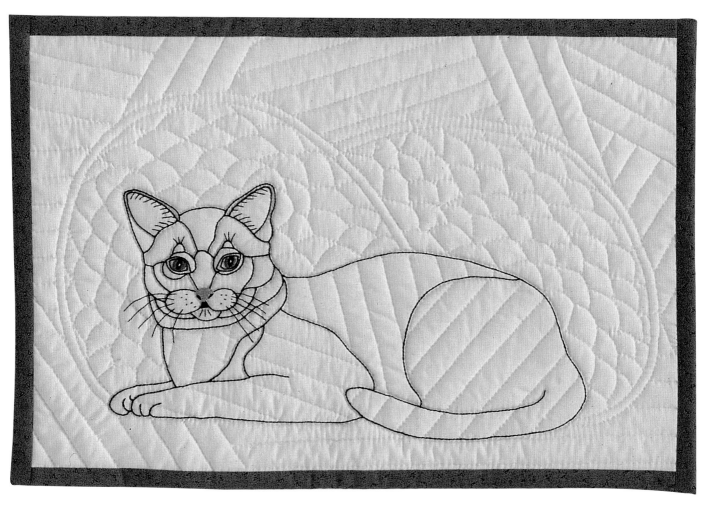

Embroidered Cat

Trace the cat design onto the background fabric using a removable marker.

DETAILS

Using two strands of black floss, stem-stitch the cat's main lines. Use a single strand of black floss for eyebrows, whiskers, muzzle dots, and ear fur. Satin-stitch the eyes, nose, and mouth. Add a white stitch to each pupil. Remove any marks. Press. Baste for quilting.

QUILTING

Quilt around the cat's key lines. Use masking tape for even spacing and quilt parallel lines inside the cat, varying the direction in different sections. Quilt two partial circles above the cat, filling in those spaces with random shells. Use more parallel lines to fill the remaining spaces, varying direction from time to time.

Remove basting and trim to approximately 19" x 13". Bind, measuring the piece for the exact length of binding strips before you stitch (see page 26).

Painted Cat

Draw the cat design onto the background fabric with a black Pigma pen.

DETAILS

Paint the cat as you like. Play with some paint on a scrap of fabric to get the feel of the technique if you are new to it. Redraw the black lines that were covered by paint. Baste for quilting, avoiding the painted areas.

QUILTING

Quilt around the cat and around random body parts for definition. Lightly mark some random hearts; and echo-quilt outward from the cat and hearts. Remove basting. Trim to approximately 15" x 10½". Bind, measuring the piece for the exact length of binding strips before you stitch (see page 26).

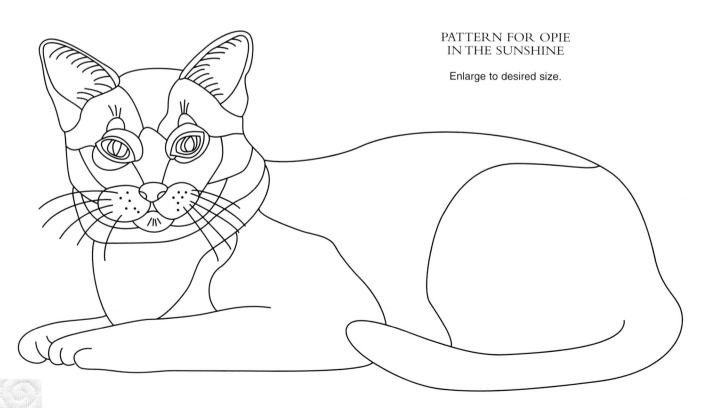

PATTERN FOR OPIE
IN THE SUNSHINE

Enlarge to desired size.

ABOUT THE AUTHOR

Carol Armstrong taught herself to quilt in 1980, developing a unique and highly artistic style. She uses her favorite technique, "Lightbox Appliqué." Botanically correct conventionalized celebrations of flora, birds, and woodland creatures are her strongest output, though any subject that catches her artistic eye may end up a minutely detailed grace on fabric.

In 1986 Carol moved to Michigan's Upper Peninsula, where she lives with her cabinetmaker husband, J.M. Friedrich, in the country near Shingleton. Carol says the wonderfully snowy winters give her time to do lots of quilting while her husband "Red" makes fine craft items in his workshop a path away. When her fingers and eyes need a diversion, there is always water to pump and bring in the house, wood to load in the woodbox, bird feeders to fill, or the large organic vegetable garden to tend.

INDEX

OTHER FINE BOOKS FROM C&T PUBLISHING:

3-in-1 Color Tool, Joen Wolfrom

250 Continuous-Line Quilting Designs for Hand, Machine & Long-Arm Quilters, Laura Lee Fritz

250 More Continuous-Line Quilting Designs for Hand, Machine & Long-Arm Quilting, Laura Lee Fritz

Along the Garden Path: More Quilters and Their Gardens, Jean Wells and Valori Wells

America from the Heart: Quilters Remember September 11, 2001

Appliqué 12 Easy Ways! Charming Quilts, Giftable Projects & Timeless Techniques, Elly Sienkiewicz

The Art of Classic Quiltmaking, Harriet Hargrave and Sharyn Craig

Baltimore Beauties and Beyond (Volume I), Elly Sienkiewicz

The Best of Baltimore Beauties, Elly Sienkiewicz

Block Magic: Over 50 Fun & Easy Blocks from Squares and Rectangles, Nancy Johnson-Srebro

A Bouquet of Quilts: Garden-Inspired Projects for the Home, edited by Jennifer Rounds & Cyndy Lyle Rymer

Butterflies & Blooms: Designs for Appliqué & Quilting, Carol Armstrong

Come Listen to My Quilts •Playful Projects •Mix & Match Designs, Kristina Becker

Elegant Stitches: An Illustrated Stitch Guide & Source Book of Inspiration, Judith Baker Montano

Enchanted Views: Quilts Inspired by Wrought-Iron Designs, Dilys A. Fronks

Exploring Machine Trapunto: New Dimensions, Hari Walner

The Fabric Stamping Handbook•Fun Projects •Tips & Tricks •Unlimited Possibilities, Jean Ray Laury

Fancy Appliqué: 12 Lessons to Enhance Your Skills, Elly Sienkiewicz

Fantastic Fabric Folding: Innovative Quilting Projects, Rebecca Wat

Free-Style Quilts: A "No Rules" Approach, Susan Carlson

Hand Appliqué with Alex Anderson: Seven Projects for Hand Appliqué, Alex Anderson

Hand Quilting with Alex Anderson: Six Projects for Hand Quilters, Alex Anderson

Heirloom Machine Quilting, 3rd ed., Harriet Hargrave

Imagery on Fabric: A Complete Surface Design Handbook, 2nd ed., Jean Ray Laury

Kids Start Quilting with Alex Anderson, Alex Anderson

Laurel Burch Quilts: Kindred Creatures, Laurel Burch

Lone Star Quilts and Beyond: Projects and Inspiration, Jan Krentz

Mastering Machine Appliqué, 2nd ed., Harriet Hargrave

Paper Piecing Picnic: Fun-Filled Projects for Every Quilter, Quilter's Newsletter Magazine

Paper Piecing with Alex Anderson, Alex Anderson

Patchwork Persuasion: Fascinating Quilts from Traditional Designs, Joen Wolfrom

The Photo Transfer Handbook: Snap It, Print It, Stitch It!, Jean Ray Laury

Pieced Flowers, Ruth B. McDowell

Pieced Vegetables, Ruth B. McDowell

Piecing: Expanding the Basics, Ruth B. McDowell

Provence Quilts and Cuisine, Marie-Christine Flocard and Cosabeth Parriaud

Quick Quilts for the Holidays: 11 Projects to Stamp, Stencil, and Sew, Trice Boerens

Quilt Lovers' Favorites, American Patchwork & Quilting

Quilting Back to Front: Fun & Easy No-Mark Techniques, Larraine Scouler

Quilting with Carol Armstrong: 30 Quilting Patterns, Appliqué Designs, 16 Projects, Carol Armstrong

Quilts, Quilts, and More Quilts! Diana McClun and Laura Nownes

Shadow Redwork with Alex Anderson: 24 Designs to Mix and Match, Alex Anderson

Show Me How to Machine Quilt: A Fun, No-Mark Approach, Kathy Sandbach

Simply Stars: Quilts that Sparkle, Alex Anderson

Start Quilting with Alex Anderson, 2nd ed.: Six Projects for First-Time Quilters, Alex Anderson

A Thimbleberries Housewarming:22 Projects for Quilters, Lynette Jensen

Wild Birds: Designs for Appliqué & Quilting, Carol Armstrong

Wildflowers: Designs for Appliqué & Quilting, Carol Armstrong

---

Note: Fabrics used in the quilts shown may not be currently available since fabric manufacturers keep most fabrics in print for only a short time.

For more information write for a free catalog:
C&T Publishing, Inc.
P.O. Box 1456
Lafayette, CA 94549
(800) 284-1114
e-mail: ctinfo@ctpub.com
website: www.ctpub.com

For quilting supplies:
Cotton Patch Mail Order
3405 Hall Lane, Dept. CTB
Lafayette, CA 94549
(800) 835-4418
(925) 283-7883
e-mail: quiltusa@yahoo.com
website: www.quiltusa.com